KU-302-939

Somebody
Loves You

By Helen Steiner Rice

Somebody Loves You

Helen Steiner Rice

Hutchinson of London

Hutchinson & Co (Publishers) Ltd
3 Fitzroy Square, London W1P 6JD

London Melbourne Sydney Auckland
Wellington Johannesburg and agencies
throughout the world

First published in Great Britain 1978
© Fleming H. Revell Company 1976

Printed and bound in Singapore

ISBN 0 09 132920 5

Contents

Introduction

The MIRACLE of MIRACLES to me
Is that GOD loves YOU and HE loves ME, too,
And through HIS love I can share with you
HIS words which I use in the poems I write,
For "HE is THE WAY and THE TRUTH and THE
LIGHT" . . .
And then through HIS love we communicate,
For we work as a BLESSED TRIUMVIRATE,
For my work is a "PARTNERSHIP of THREE"—
GOD first, then YOU, and last of all ME . . .
For nothing I write is outstanding or great
Until it is "PART of HIS TRIUMVIRATE"!

Helen Steiner Rice

FOREWORD

During the preparation of the manuscript for this book, Mrs.
Rice has endured a severe and difficult illness. Recently
we were privileged to receive the following poem from her, written
while she was in the hospital. It was not intended for this
book, but rather as a message to her friends at Revell and
elsewhere. Because it meant so much to us we have secured her
permission to share it with her readers. This also seems
an appropriate time for us at Revell to express how privileged
we feel to be able to work with her.

THE PUBLISHERS

My Birthday in Bethesda

How little we know what GOD has in store
As daily HE blesses our lives more and more . . .
I've lived many years and learned many things,
But today I have grown "NEW SPIRITUAL WINGS,"
For pain has a way of broadening our view
And bringing us closer in sympathy, too,
To those who are living in constant pain
And trying somehow to bravely sustain
The faith and endurance to keep on trying
When they almost welcome "the peace of dying" . . . .
And without this experience I would have lived and died
Without fathoming the pain of CHRIST crucified,
For none of us know what pain's all about
Until our "SPIRITUAL WINGS" start to sprout . . .
So thank YOU, GOD, for the "GIFT" YOU sent
To teach me that pain is HEAVEN-SENT.

May 19, 1976

11

Somebody
Loves You

Somebody Loves You

SOMEBODY LOVES YOU more than you know,
SOMEBODY GOES WITH YOU wherever you go,
SOMEBODY REALLY and TRULY CARES,
And LOVINGLY LISTENS TO ALL OF YOUR
PRAYERS . . .

Don't doubt for a minute
     that this is not true,
For GOD loves HIS CHILDREN
     and takes care of them, too. . .
And all of HIS TREASURES
     are yours to share
If you love HIM completely
     and show HIM you care. . .
And if you "WALK IN HIS FOOTSTEPS"
     and have the FAITH to BELIEVE,
There's nothing you ask for
     that you will not receive!

He Loves You

It's amazing and incredible,
But it's as true as it can be,
God loves and understands us all
And that means YOU and ME—
His grace is all sufficient
For both the YOUNG and OLD,
For the lonely and the timid,
For the brash and for the bold—
His love knows no exceptions,
So never feel excluded,
No matter WHO or WHAT you are
Your name has been included—
And no matter what your past has been,
Trust God to understand,
And no matter what your problem is
Just place it in His Hand—
For in all of our UNLOVELINESS
This GREAT GOD LOVES US STILL,
He loved us since the world began
And what's more, HE ALWAYS WILL!

God's Love

GOD'S LOVE is like an island
In life's ocean vast and wide—
A peaceful, quiet shelter
From the restless, rising tide. . .

GOD' LOVE is like an anchor
When the angry billows roll—
A mooring in the storms of life,
A stronghold for the soul. . .

GOD'S LOVE is like a fortress
And we seek protection there
When the waves of tribulation
Seem to drown us in despair. . .

GOD'S LOVE is like a harbor
Where our souls can find sweet rest
From the struggle and the tension
Of life's fast and futile quest. . .

GOD'S LOVE is like a beacon
Burning bright with FAITH and PRAYER
And through the changing scenes of life
We can find a HAVEN THERE!

Enfolded in His Love

The LOVE of GOD surrounds us
Like the air we breathe around us—
As near as a heartbeat,
        as close as a prayer,
And whenever we need HIM
        HE'LL always be there!

One Thing Never Changes

The seasons swiftly come and go
And with them comes the thought
Of all the various changes
That time in flight has brought. . .
But one thing never changes,
It remains the same forever,
GOD truly loves "HIS CHILDREN"
And HE will forsake them never!

My God Is No Stranger

God is no stranger in a faraway place,
He's as close as the wind that blows cross my face,
It's true I can't see the wind as it blows
But I feel it around me and my heart surely knows
That God's mighty Hand can be felt every minute
For there is nothing on earth that God isn't in it—
The sky and the stars, the waves and the sea,
The dew on the grass, the leaves on a tree
Are constant reminders of God and His nearness,
Proclaiming His Presence with crystal-like clearness—
So how could I think God was far, far away
When I feel Him beside me every hour of the day,
And I've plenty of reasons to know God's My Friend
And this is one Friendship that time cannot end!

Wondrous Evidence

Who can see the dawn break through
    without a glimpse of HEAVEN and YOU. . .
For who but GOD could make the day
    and gently put the night away.

The Mystery and Miracle of His Creative Hand

In the beauty of a snowflake,
Falling softly on the land,
Is the MYSTERY and the MIRACLE
Of GOD'S GREAT, CREATIVE HAND!

The Reflections of God

The silent stars in timeless skies,
The wonderment in children's eyes,
The autumn haze, the breath of spring,
The chirping song the crickets sing,
A rosebud in a slender vase
Are all reflections of GOD's FACE.

"Seek Ye First the Kingdom of God"

Always remember
     that whatever betide you
THE POWER of GOD
     is always beside you,
And if friends disappoint you
     and plans go astray
And nothing works out
     in just the right way
And you feel you have failed
     in achieving your goal
And that life wrongly placed you
     in an unfitting role,
Take heart and "stand tall"
     and think who you are,
For GOD is YOUR FATHER
     and no one can bar

Or keep you from reaching
    your desired success
Or withhold the joy
    that is yours to possess. . .
For with GOD on your side
    it matters not who
Is working to keep
    life's good things from you,
For you need nothing more
    than GOD'S GUIDANCE and LOVE
To insure you the things
    that you're most worthy of . . .
So trust in HIS WISDOM
    and follow HIS WAYS
And be not concerned
    with the world's empty praise,
But SEEK FIRST HIS KINGDOM
    and you will possess
The world's greatest riches
    which is true happiness.

Our Refuge
and Strength

THE LORD is OUR SALVATION
And OUR STRENGTH in every fight,
OUR REDEEMER and PROTECTOR,
OUR ETERNAL GUIDING LIGHT. . .
HE has promised to sustain us,
HE'S OUR REFUGE from all harms,
And underneath this refuge
Are THE EVERLASTING ARMS!

God's Presence Is Ever Beside You

And so today I walk with GOD
Because I love HIM so. . .
If I have FAITH and TRUST in HIM,
There's nothing I need know!

God's Hand Is Always There

I am perplexed and often vexed
And sometimes I cry and sadly sigh,
But do not think, DEAR FATHER ABOVE,
I question YOU or YOUR UNCHANGING LOVE—
It's just sometimes when I reach out
YOU seem to be nowhere about. . .
And while I'm sure that YOU love me still
And I know in my heart that YOU ALWAYS WILL,
Somehow I feel that I cannot reach YOU
And though I get down on my knees and beseech YOU,
I cannot bring YOU closer to me
And I feel adrift on life's raging sea. . .
But though I cannot find YOUR HAND
To lead me on to THE PROMISED LAND,
I still believe with all my being
YOUR HAND IS THERE BEYOND MY SEEING!

Faith Is the Key to Heaven

Oh, FATHER, grant once more to men
A SIMPLE, CHILDLIKE FAITH again,
Forgetting COLOR, RACE, and CREED
And seeing only the heart's deep need. . .
For FAITH alone can save man's soul
And lead him to a HIGHER GOAL,
For there's but one unfailing course—
We win by FAITH and NOT by FORCE.

Live by Faith
and Not by Feelings

When everything is pleasant and bright
And the things we do turn out just right,
We feel without question that GOD is real,
For, when we are happy, how good we feel. . .
But when the tides turn and gone is the song
And misfortune comes and our plans go wrong,
Doubt creeps in and we start to wonder
And our thoughts about GOD are torn asunder—
For we feel deserted in time of deep stress,
Without GOD'S PRESENCE to assure us and bless. . .
And it is then when our senses are reeling
We realize clearly it's FAITH and not FEELING—
For it takes GREAT FAITH to patiently wait,
Believing "GOD comes NOT TOO SOON or TOO LATE."

"Trust" Is a "Must"

"I have no FAITH," the skeptic cries,
"I can only accept what I see with my eyes" . . .
Yet man has to have FAITH or he would never complete
Just a simple task like crossing the street,
For he has to have FAITH in his manly stride
To get him across to the other side,
And the world would be panic-stricken indeed
If no one thought that he could succeed
In doing the smallest, simplest thing
That life with its many demands can bring. . .
So why do the skeptics still ridicule
And call "THE MAN of FAITH" a fool
When FAITH is the BASIS of all that we do—
And that includes UNBELIEVERS, too.

God Is Everywhere

We cannot go beyond GOD'S reach
  or beyond HIS love and care,
For we are all a PART of GOD
  and GOD is EVERYWHERE!

The Master Builder

GOD is THE MASTER BUILDER,
HIS PLANS are perfect and true,
And when HE sends you sorrow
It's part of HIS PLAN for you. . .
For all things work together
To complete THE MASTER PLAN
And GOD up in HIS HEAVEN
Can see what's best for man.

Life Is a Highway

LIFE is a HIGHWAY
      on which the years go by. . .
Sometimes the ROAD is LEVEL,
      sometimes the HILLS are HIGH. . .
But as we travel onward
      to a future that's unknown
We can make EACH MILE we travel
      a "HEAVENLY STEPPING-STONE"!

"Love Divine,
All Love Excelling"

In a myriad of miraculous ways
GOD shapes our lives and changes our days,
Beyond our will or even knowing
GOD keeps our spirit ever growing. . .
For LIGHTS and SHADOWS, SUN and RAIN,
SADNESS and GLADNESS, JOY and PAIN,
Combine to make our lives complete
And give us VICTORY through DEFEAT. . .
"Oh, Love Divine, All Love Excelling,"
In troubled hearts YOU just keep dwelling,
Patiently waiting for a "PRODIGAL SON"
To say at last, "THY WILL BE DONE."

Today, Tomorrow, and Always He Is There

In sickness or health,
In suffering and pain,
In storm-laden skies,
In sunshine and rain,
GOD ALWAYS IS THERE
To lighten your way
And lead you through "darkness"
To a much brighter day.

A Time of Renewal and Spiritual Blessing

No one likes to be sick
     and yet we know
It takes sunshine and rain
     to make flowers grow. . .
And if we never were sick
     and never felt pain,
We'd be like a desert
     without any rain,
And who wants a life
     that is barren and dry
With never a "cloud"
     to "darken the sky" . . .
For "continuous sun"
     goes unrecognized
Like the blessings GOD sends
     which are often disguised,
For sometimes a sickness
     that seems so distressing
Is a "time of renewal"
     and a "spiritual blessing."

Are You Physically Ill or Soul Sick?

Sometimes when we are
    physically ill
We're prone to resort
    to a tonic or pill,
Neglecting to place
    ourselves in GOD'S CARE
By seeking HIS help
    on "THE WINGS OF PRAYER"—
For GOD can remove
    our uncertain fear
And replace our worry
    with healing cheer. . .
So close your eyes
    and open your heart
And let GOD come in
    and freely impart
A brighter outlook
    and new courage, too,
As HIS "spiritual sunshine"
    smiles on you.

How Little We Know
of Suffering and Woe

GOD, how little I was really aware
Of the pain and the trouble and deep despair
That floods the hearts of those in pain
As they struggle to cope but feel it's in vain,
Crushed with frustration and with "no haven to seek,"
With broken spirits and bodies so weak. . .
And yet they forget CHRIST suffered and died
And hung on the cross and was crucified,
And HE did it all so some happy day,
When the sorrows of earth have all passed away,
We who have suffered will forever be free
To live with GOD in ETERNITY!

"In God Is My Strength"

"Love Divine, All Love Excelling"
Makes my "humbled heart" YOUR DWELLING,
For without YOUR LOVE DIVINE
Total darkness would be mine,
My earthly load I could not bear
If YOU were not there to share
All the pain, despair, and sorrow
That almost makes me dread tomorrow,
For I am often weak and weary
And life is dark and bleak and dreary. . . .
But somehow when I realize
That HE who made the sea and skies
And holds the whole world in HIS HAND
Has my "small soul" in HIS COMMAND,
It gives me STRENGTH to try once more
To somehow reach "THE HEAVENLY DOOR"
Where I will LIVE FOREVERMORE
With friends and loved ones I adore!

God's Tender Care

When trouble comes,
        as it does to us all,
God is so great
        and we are so small—
But there is nothing
        that we need know
If we have faith
        that wherever we go
God will be waiting
        to help us bear
Our pain and sorrow,
        our suffering and care—
For no pain or suffering
        is ever too much
To yield itself
        to God's merciful touch!

We Never Walk Alone

What more can we ask of the SAVIOUR
Than to know we are never alone—
That HIS MERCY and LOVE are unfailing
And HE makes all our problems HIS OWN.

In God We Are Secure

FAITH makes it wholly possible
    to quietly endure
The violent world around us
    for in GOD we are secure.

People's Problems

EVERYONE has problems
        in this restless world of care,
EVERYONE grows weary
        with the "cross they have to bear,"
EVERYONE is troubled
        and "their skies are overcast"
As they try to face the future
        while still dwelling in the past . . .
But the people with their problems
        only "listen with one ear"
For people only listen
        to the things they want to hear

And they only hear the kind of things
    they are able to believe
And the ANSWERS that are God's to give
    they're not ready to receive,
So while the PEOPLE'S PROBLEMS
    keep growing every day
And man vainly tries to solve them
    in his own self-willful way. . .
God seeks to help and watches,
    waiting always patiently
To help them solve their problems
    whatever they may be—
So may the people of all nations
    at last become aware
That God will solve the PEOPLE'S PROBLEMS
    through FAITH and HOPE and PRAYER!

God's Assurance
Gives Us Endurance

My blessings are so many,
My troubles are so few,
How can I feel discouraged
When I know that I have YOU
And I have the "SWEET ASSURANCE"
That I'll never stand alone
If I but keep remembering
I am YOURS and YOURS ALONE. . .
So, in this world of trouble
With "darkness" all around,
Take my hand and lead me
Until I stand on "HIGHER GROUND"
And help me to endure the "storms"
That keep raging deep inside me
And make me more aware each day
That no evil can betide me
If I remain undaunted
Though the "billows sweep and roll,"
Knowing I have YOUR ASSURANCE
There's a HAVEN for MY SOUL,
For ANYTHING and EVERYTHING
Can somehow be endured
If YOUR PRESENCE is beside me
And LOVINGLY ASSURED!

This Is Just
a Resting Place

Sometimes the road of life seems long
      as we travel through the years
And, with a heart that's broken
      and eyes brimful of tears,
We falter in our weariness
      and sink beside the way,
But GOD leans down and whispers,
      "Child, there'll be another day"—
And the road will grow much smoother
      and much easier to face,
So do not be disheartened—
      this is just a "RESTING PLACE."

Put Your Problem in God's Hands, for He Completely Understands

Although it sometimes seems to us
     our prayers have not been heard,
GOD always knows our every need
     without a single word. . .
And HE will not forsake us
     even though the way seems steep,
For always HE is near to us
     a tender watch to keep. . .
And in good time HE'LL answer us
     and in HIS love HE'LL send
GREATER THINGS THAN WE HAVE ASKED
     and BLESSINGS WITHOUT END. . .
So though we do not understand
     why trouble comes to man
Can we not be contented
     just to know that IT'S GOD'S PLAN.

Put Your Soul in God's Control

Many trials and troubles
Are scattered on our way,
Daily little crosses
Are a part of every day. . .
But the troubles we have suffered
Are over, passed, and through,
So why should bygone happenings
Keep on gravely troubling you . . .
And the problems that beset us
In the NOW and PRESENT HOUR
We need not try to solve alone
Without GOD'S GRACE and POWER
And those scheduled for tomorrow
Still belong to GOD ALONE—
They are still unborn and formless
And a part of the unknown. . .
So let us face the trouble
That is ours this present minute
And count on GOD to help us
And put HIS MERCY in it
And forget the past and future
And dwell wholly on today,
For GOD controls the future
And HE will direct our way.

Be Not Dismayed
By Dismal Days

It's a dismal, dreary morning
     and as I sometimes do
I feel a little dreary
     and kinda downcast, too,
For let nobody tell you
     that life's a "happy song"
And that we just keep smiling
     when everything goes wrong. . .
For it just would not be natural
     to always wear a smile,
For a smile would be a "silly grin"
     if it covered up a trial. . .

For there are certain periods
  when the soul is "sweetly sad"
As it contemplates the mystery
  of both good times and bad. . .
We're not really discontented
  and we are never unaware
That THE GOOD LORD UP IN HEAVEN
  HAS US ALWAYS IN HIS CARE,
But the soul of man is restless
  and it just keeps longing for
A HAVEN that is SAFE and SURE
  that will last FOREVERMORE. . .
And as I sit here writing this
  a thought passed through my mind—
"Why dwell on PAST or FUTURE
  or WHAT'S AHEAD or GONE BEHIND?"
Just follow GOD unquestioningly
  because YOU LOVE HIM SO,
For if you trust HIS JUDGMENT
  THERE IS NOTHING YOU NEED KNOW!

My Daily Prayer

GOD, be MY RESTING PLACE and MY
       PROTECTION
In hours of trouble, defeat, and dejection. . .
May I never give way to self-pity and sorrow,
May I always be sure of a better tomorrow,
May I stand undaunted come what may
Secure in the knowledge I have only to pray
And ask MY CREATOR and FATHER ABOVE
To keep me serene in HIS GRACE and HIS LOVE!

Build a Firm
Foundation of Faith

FAITH is a force that is greater
Than knowledge or power or skill. . .
And the darkest defeat turns to triumph
If we trust in GOD'S WISDOM and WILL.

If We But Believe

If we put our problems in GOD'S HAND,
There is nothing we need understand. . .
It is enough to just believe
That what we need we will receive.

Trust and Believe
and You Will Receive

Whatever our problems, troubles, and sorrows,
If we trust in THE LORD, there'll be BRIGHTER TOMORROWS,
For there's nothing too much for THE GREAT GOD to do,
And all that HE asks or expects from you
Is FAITH that's unshaken by tribulations and tears
That keeps growing stronger along with the years,
Content in the knowledge that GOD knows best
And that trouble and sorrow are only a test—
For without GOD'S testing of our soul
It never would reach its ultimate goal. . .
So keep on believing, whatever betide you,
Knowing that GOD will be with you to guide you,
And all that HE PROMISED will be yours to receive
If you TRUST HIM COMPLETELY and ALWAYS BELIEVE.

He Answers All
Our Needs

There's no problem too big
  and no question too small,
Just ask GOD in FAITH
  and HE'LL answer them all—
Not always at once,
  so be patient and wait,
For "GOD never comes
  TOO SOON or TOO LATE"—
So·trust in HIS WISDOM
  and believe in HIS WORD,
Fo no prayer's unanswered
  and no prayer unheard.

"With God
All Things Are Possible"

Nothing is ever too hard to do
If your FAITH is STRONG and your PURPOSE is TRUE. .
So "NEVER GIVE UP" and NEVER STOP
Just "JOURNEY ON to THE MOUNTAINTOP"!

Try It! It Works!

Stop wishing for things
    you complain you have not
And start making the BEST
    of all that you've got.

God, Grant Me. . .

COURAGE and HOPE
     for every day,
FAITH to guide me
     along my way,
UNDERSTANDING
     and WISDOM, too,
And GRACE TO ACCEPT
     what life gives me to do.

Help Us to See and Understand

GOD, give us wider vision
        to see and understand
That both "the Sun and Showers"
        are gifts from THY GREAT HAND,
And when our lives are overcast
        with trouble and with care,
Give us faith to see beyond
        the dark clouds of despair,
And give us strength to rise above
        the mist of doubt and fear
And recognize the hidden smile
        behind each burning tear,

And teach us that it takes the showers
     to make the flowers grow
And only in the storms of life
     when the winds of trouble blow
Can man, too, reach maturity
     and grow in faith and grace
And gain the strength and courage
     to enable him to face
Sunny days as well as rain,
     high peaks as well as low,
Knowing that the "April Showers
     will make the May Flowers Grow"—
And then at last may we accept
     "the Sunshine and the Showers,"
Confident it takes them both
     to make Salvation ours!

Learn to Recognize
a Blessing

While it's very difficult
      for mankind to understand
GOD'S INTENTIONS and HIS PURPOSE
      and the WORKINGS of HIS HAND,
If we observe the miracles
      that happen every day,
We cannot help but be convinced
      that in HIS WONDROUS WAY
GOD makes what seemed unbearable
      and painful and distressing
Easily acceptable
      when we view it as a BLESSING.

Sorrow Helps
Our Souls to Grow

There's a lot of comfort in the thought
That sorrow, grief, and woe
Are sent into our lives sometimes
To help our souls to grow. . .
For through the depths of sorrow
Comes understanding love,
And peace and truth and comfort
Are sent from GOD ABOVE.

We Can't Have a "Crown" Without a "Cross"

We all have those days
    that are dismal and dreary
And we feel sorta blue
    and lonely and weary,
But we have to admit
    that life is worth living
And GOD gives us reasons
    for daily "THANKSGIVING". . .
For life's an experience
    GOD'S CHILDREN go through
That's made up of gladness
    and much sadness, too. . .

But we have to know both
    the "BITTER" and "SWEET"
If we want a GOOD LIFE
    that is FULL and COMPLETE,
For each trial we suffer
    and every shed tear
Just gives us NEW STRENGTH
    to PERSEVERE
As we "climb" the "STEEP HILLS"
    along LIFE'S WAY
That lead us at last
    to that WONDERFUL DAY
Where the "CROSS" we have carried
    becomes a "CROWN"
And at last we can lay
    OUR BURDEN DOWN!

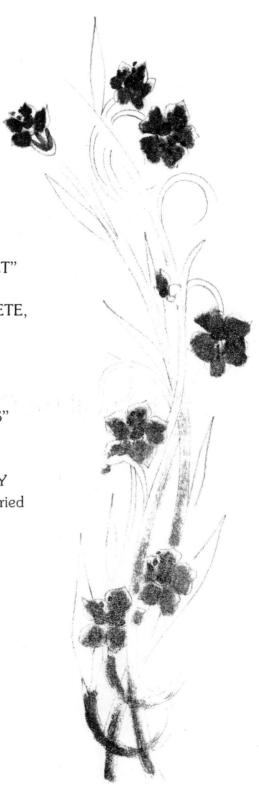

"Thy Will Be Done"

God did not promise "sun without rain,"
        "light without darkness" or "joy without pain"—
He only promised us "STRENGTH for the DAY"
        when "the darkness" comes and we lose our way,
For only through sorrow do we grow more aware
        that God is our refuge in times of despair. . . .
For when we are happy and life's bright and fair,
        we often forget to kneel down in prayer,
But God seems much closer and needed much more
        when trouble and sorrow stand outside our door—
For then we seek shelter in His wondrous love
        and we ask Him to send us help from above. . .
And that is the reason we know it is true
        that bright, shining hours and dark, sad ones, too,
Are part of the plan God made for each one,
        and all we can pray is "THY WILL BE DONE"!

God's Mighty Handiwork

"The earth is THE LORD'S
     and the fulness thereof"—
It speaks of HIS GREATNESS
     and it sings of HIS LOVE—
It whispers of mysteries
     we cannot comprehend
Of a beautiful land
     where life has no end!

Nothing Is Lost Forever

The waking earth at Springtime
      Reminds us it is true
That nothing ever really dies
      That is not born anew. . .
So trust GOD'S ALL-WISE WISDOM
      And doubt THE FATHER never,
For in HIS HEAVENLY KINGDOM
      There is NOTHING LOST FOREVER!

All Nature Tells Us
Nothing Really Ever Dies

Nothing really ever dies
That is not born anew—
The MIRACLES of NATURE
All tell us this is true. . .
The flowers sleeping peacefully
Beneath the Winter's snow
Awaken from their icy grave
When Spring winds start to blow
And little brooks and singing streams,
Icebound beneath the snow,
Begin to babble merrily
Beneath the sun's warm glow. . .
And all around on every side
New life and joy appear
To tell us NOTHING EVER DIES
And we should have no fear,
For death is just a detour
Along life's wending way
That leads GOD'S chosen children
To a bright and glorious day.

Tomorrow
I'll Think About God

Not today when I am so busy,
Not today when there's so much to do,
Not today while I'm young and eager
And life is far-reaching and new—
But tomorrow when I am older
And the tempo of life is less,
I'll have more time for praying
And for meditating, I guess. . .
But time is swift in its passing
And before we are really aware
We find ourselves growing older
And daily in need of GOD'S care. . .

And while GOD is always ready
To help us and lead us along,
Because we have tarried and wasted
Our young days in "dancing and song,"
We find we are not well acquainted
With the wonderful love of THE LORD
And we feel very strange in HIS PRESENCE
And unworthy of OUR FATHER'S REWARD—
For only the children who seek HIM
With hearts yet untouched and still clean
Can ever experience HIS GREATNESS
And know what HIS LOVE can mean. . .
So waste not the hours of "LIFE'S MORNING,"
Get acquainted with GOD when you're born,
And when you come to "LIFE'S EVENING,"
It will shine like "THE GLORY of MORN"!

Seek the Lord Continuously

IT'S NOT ENOUGH TO SAY "I BELIEVE,"
IT'S NOT ENOUGH TO ASK and RECEIVE,
IT'S NOT ENOUGH TO REPEAT THE LORD'S PRAYER,
IT'S NOT ENOUGH TO JUST SAY, "I CARE,"
IT'S NOT ENOUGH TO BE PLEASANT and KIND,
IT'S NOT ENOUGH TO KEEP GOD IN YOUR MIND,
IT'S NOT ENOUGH JUST TO FEED THE POOR,
IT'S NOT ENOUGH TO FORBEAR and ENDURE,
FOR WHILE THESE THINGS ARE ALL GOOD TO DO
THEY CANNOT INSURE SALVATION FOR YOU,
FOR NOT UNTIL YOU ARE BORN ANEW
CAN THE SPIRIT OF GOD BE ALIVE IN YOU,
FOR THE SPIRIT OF GOD WILL SOON BE DEAD
UNLESS IT IS DAILY NOURISHED and FED!

The Better You Know Him, The More You Love Him!

The better you know GOD, the better you feel,
For to learn more about HIM and discover HE'S REAL
Can wholly, completely, and miraculously change,
Reshape and remake and then rearrange
Your mixed-up, miserable, and unhappy life
"Adrift on the sea of sin-sickened strife"—
But when you once know this "MAN of GOOD WILL,"
HE will calm your life and say "PEACE, BE STILL" . . .
So open your "heart's door" and let CHRIST come in
And HE'LL give you new life and free you from sin—
And there is no joy that can ever compare
With the joy of knowing you're in GOD'S care.

There's Peace and Calm
in the Twenty-Third Psalm

With THE LORD as "YOUR SHEPHERD"
     you have all that you need,
For, if you "FOLLOW IN HIS FOOTSTEPS"
     wherever HE may lead,
HE will guard and guide and keep you
     in HIS loving, watchful care
And, when traveling in "dark valleys,"
     "YOUR SHEPHERD" will be there . . .
HIS goodness is unfailing,
     HIS kindness knows no end,
For THE LORD is a "GOOD SHEPHERD"
     on whom you can depend. . .
So, when your heart is troubled,
     you'll find quiet peace and calm
If you open up the Bible
     and just read this treasured Psalm.

Begin Each Day
by Kneeling to Pray

Start every day
      with a "Good Morning" prayer
And GOD will bless each thing you do
      and keep you in HIS CARE. . .
And never, never sever
      the "SPIRIT'S SILKEN STRAND"
That OUR FATHER up in HEAVEN
      holds in HIS MIGHTY HAND!

The Heavenly Staircase

Prayers are the stairs that lead to God,
And there's joy every step of the way
When we make our pilgrimage to HIM
With love in our hearts each day.

"The House of Prayer"

"THE HOUSE of PRAYER" is no farther away
Than the quiet spot where you kneel and pray,
For the heart is a temple when GOD is there
As you place yourself in HIS LOVING CARE.

My Garden of Prayer

My garden beautifies my yard
  and adds fragrance to the air. . . .
But it is also MY CATHEDRAL
  and MY QUIET PLACE OF PRAYER. . .
So little do we realize
  that "THE GLORY and THE POWER"
Of HE who made the UNIVERSE
  lies hidden in a flower.

Finding Faith in a Flower

Sometimes when faith is running low
And I cannot fathom WHY THINGS ARE SO. . .
I walk alone among the flowers I grow
And learn the "ANSWERS" to ALL I WOULD KNOW. . .
For among my flowers I have come to see
Life's MIRACLE and its MYSTERY. . .
And standing in silence and reverie
My FAITH COMES FLOODING BACK TO ME!

The Answer

In the tiny petal
      of a tiny flower
            that grew from a tiny pod
Is the MIRACLE
      and the MYSTERY
         of ALL CREATION and GOD!

Learn to Rest
So Your Life Will Be Blest

We all need "short vacations"
  in life's fast and maddening race—
An interlude of quietness
  from the constant, jet-age pace. . .
So, when your day is pressure-packed
  and your hours are all too few,
Just close your eyes and meditate
  and let GOD talk to you,
For, when we keep on pushing,
  we're not following in GOD'S WAY—
We are foolish, selfish robots
  mechanized to fill each day

With unimportant trivia
        that makes life more complex
And gives us greater problems
        to irritate and vex. . .
So, when your nervous network
        becomes a tangled mess,
Just close your eyes in silent prayer
        and ask THE LORD to bless
Each thought that you are thinking,
        each decision you must make,
As well as every word you speak
        and every step you take,
For only by the grace of GOD
        can we gain self-control
And only meditative thoughts
        can restore your "PEACE OF SOUL."

Life Can't Always Be a Song
—You Have to Have Trouble to Make You Strong. . .

So whenever you are troubled
And everything goes wrong,
It is just GOD working in you
To make YOUR SPIRIT STRONG!

The Best Medication
Is Meditation

If your "soul is sick"
     and your "heart is sad"
And the good things in life
     begin to look bad,
Don't be too sure
     that you're physically ill
And run to the doctor
     for a sedative pill. . .
For nothing can heal
     a "soul that is sick"
Or guarantee a cure
     as complete and quick
As a heart-to-heart talk
     with GOD and HIS SON,
Who on the shores of the Galilee
     just said "THY WILL BE DONE". . .
So, when you're feeling downcast,
     seek GOD in MEDITATION,
For a little talk with JESUS
     is unfailing MEDICATION.

Daily Prayers
Dissolve Your Cares

I meet God in the morning
And go with Him through the day,
Then in the stillness of the night
Before sleep comes I pray
That God will just "take over"
All the problems I couldn't solve
And in the peacefulness of sleep
My cares will all dissolve,
So when I open my eyes
To greet another day
I'll find myself renewed in strength
And there'll open up a way
To meet what seemed impossible
For me to solve alone
And once again I'll be assured
I am never "ON MY OWN". . .

For if we try to stand alone
We are weak and we will fall,
For God is always GREATEST
When we're helpless, lost, and small,
And no day is unmeetable
If on rising our first thought
Is to thank God for the blessings
That His loving care has brought. . .
So meet Him in the morning
And go with Him through the day
And thank Him for His guidance
Each evening when you pray,
And if you follow faithfully
This daily way to pray
You will never in your lifetime
Face another "hopeless day."

Anxious Prayers

When we are deeply disturbed with a problem
And our mind is filled with doubt
And we struggle to find a solution
But there seems to be no way out,
We futilely keep on trying
To untangle our web of distress—
But our own little, puny efforts
Meet with very little success. . .
And finally exhausted and weary,
Discouraged and downcast and low,
With no foreseeable answer
And with no other place to go,
We kneel down in sheer desperation
And slowly and stumblingly pray
Then impatiently wait for an answer
Which we fully expect right away. . .

And then, when GOD does not answer,
In one, sudden instant we say,
"GOD does not seem to be listening,
So why should we bother to pray" . . .
But GOD can't get through to "THE ANXIOUS"
Who are much too impatient to wait—
You have to believe in GOD'S PROMISE
That HE COMES NOT TOO SOON or TOO LATE,
For, whether GOD answers promptly
Or delays in answering your prayer,
YOU MUST HAVE FAITH TO BELIEVE HIM
And TO KNOW IN YOUR HEART HE'LL BE THERE. . .
So be not impatient or hasty,
Just TRUST in THE LORD and BELIEVE,
For whatever you ask in FAITH and LOVE
In abundance you are sure to RECEIVE.

Make It a Two-Way Prayer

You're troubled and worried,
  you don't know what to do,
So you seek GOD in prayer
  and HE listens to you,
But you seldom pause
  to let GOD speak—
You just want the answer
  that you desperately seek. . .
And after you've pleaded,
  you don't give GOD a chance
To discuss the best way
  to meet your circumstance
And you really miss
  the best part of prayer—
Which is feeling and knowing
  GOD'S PRESENCE IS THERE. . .

For so few of us linger
          to quietly share
The "SILENT COMMUNION"
          that fills the air
In which GOD is speaking
          and telling us why
Sometimes there's no answer
          to our immediate cry. . .
So pause for a while
          and just silently wait
And give GOD a chance
          to communicate,
For TWO-WAY PRAYER
          forms a JOYOUS RELATION
When we listen to GOD
          in "SHARED MEDITATION."

This Is My Prayer

Bless me, heavenly Father,
      forgive my erring ways,
Grant me strength to serve Thee,
      put purpose in my days. . .
Give me understanding
      enough to make me kind
So I may judge all people
      with my heart and not my mind. . .
And teach me to be patient
      in everything I do,
Content to trust Your Wisdom
      and to follow after You. . .
And help me when I falter
      and hear me when I pray
And receive me in Thy Kingdom
      to dwell with Thee some day.

Faith Is a Candle

In this sick world of hatred
And violence and sin,
Where men renounce morals
And reject discipline,
We stumble in "darkness"
Groping vainly for "light"
To distinguish the difference
Between Wrong and Right,
But Dawn cannot follow
This Night of Despair
Unless Faith Lights a Candle
In All Hearts Everywhere
And warmed by the glow
Our hate melts away
And Love Lights The Path
To a Peaceful, New Day.

"Is Life Worth Living?"

The GREAT and SMALL. . .the GOOD and BAD,
The YOUNG and OLD. . .the SAD and GLAD
Are asking today, "IS LIFE WORTH LIVING?"
And the ANSWER is only in LOVING and GIVING—
For only LOVE can make man KIND
And KINDNESS of HEART brings PEACE of MIND.

Widen My Vision

God, open my eyes
    so I may see
And feel Your presence
    close to me. . .
Give me strength
    for my stumbling feet
As I battle the crowd
    on life's busy street,
And widen the vision
    of my unseeing eyes
So in passing faces
    I'll recognize
Not just a stranger,
    unloved and unknown,
But a friend with a heart
    that is much like my own. . .
Give me perception
    to make me aware
That scattered profusely
    on life's thoroughfare
Are the best GIFTS of GOD
    that we daily pass by
As we look at the world
    with an UNSEEING EYE.

Unaware, We Pass Him By

On life's busy thoroughfares
We meet with angels unawares—
But we are too busy to listen or hear,
Too busy to sense that God is near,
Too busy to stop and recognize
The grief that lies in another's eyes,
Too busy to offer to help or share,
Too busy to sympathize or care,
Too busy to do the good things we should,
Telling ourselves we would if we could. . .
But life is too swift and the pace is too great
And we dare not pause for we might be late
For our next appointment which means so much,
We are willing to brush off the Saviour's touch,
And we tell ourselves there will come a day
We will have more time to pause on our way. . .
But before we know it "life's sun has set"
And we've passed the Saviour but never met,
For hurrying along life's thoroughfare
We passed Him by and remained unaware
That within the very sight of our eye,
Unnoticed, the Son of God passed by.

In Reverent Reverie
God Came to Me

I sat among the people
>in the church of my childhood and youth. . .

I came back to sing the songs of praise
>and to hear "the words of truth". . .

I looked into the faces
>of the young folks and the old. . .

And listened, as I used to,
>to "THE SWEETEST STORY EVER TOLD". . .

I had come back home to visit
>and to meet friends in glad reunion. . .

But the Sunday that I went to church
>turned out to be "COMMUNION". . .

And so it was, when I arose
>from my "COMMUNION PRAYER". . .

I no longer saw JUST FACES,
>for GOD was standing there.

Quit Supposin'!

If you desire to be HAPPY,
Don't think of the things that you dread—
Just give up "SUPPOSIN' THE WORST THINGS"
And look for "THE BEST THINGS" instead!

Be of Good Cheer

Since fear and dread and worry
Cannot help in any way,
It's much healthier and happier
To be cheerful every day—
And if we'll only try it
We will find, without a doubt,
A cheerful attitude's something
No one should be without—
For when the heart is cheerful
It cannot be filled with fear,
And without fear the way ahead
Seems more distinct and clear—
And we realize there's nothing
We need ever face alone,
For OUR HEAVENLY FATHER loves us
And our problems are HIS OWN.

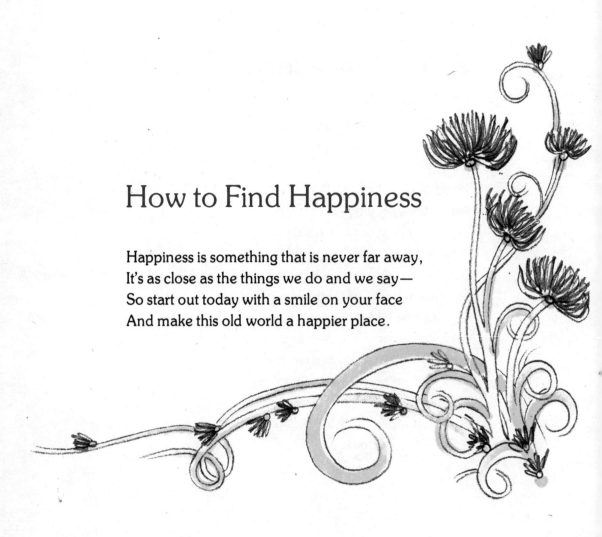

How to Find Happiness

Happiness is something that is never far away,
It's as close as the things we do and we say—
So start out today with a smile on your face
And make this old world a happier place.

The Joy
of Unselfish Giving

Time is not measured
     by the years that you live
But by the deeds that you do
     and the joy that you give—
And each day as it comes
     brings a chance to each one
To love to the fullest,
     leaving nothing undone
That would brighten the life
     or lighten the load
Of some weary traveler
     lost on Life's Road—
So what does it matter
     how long we may live
If as long as we live
     we unselfishly give.

Not by the Years We Live
But How Much We Give

From one day to another
      GOD will gladly give
To everyone who seeks HIM
      and tries each day to live
A little bit more closely
      to GOD and to each other,
Seeing everyone who passes
      as a neighbor, friend, or brother,
Not only joy and happiness
      but the faith to meet each trial
Not with fear and trepidation
      but with an "inner smile"—
For we know life's never measured
      by how many years we live
But by the kindly things we do
      and the happiness we give.

It's Such a Busy World!

Our days are so crowded
        and our hours are so few
And there's so little time
        and so much to do
That the days fly by
        and are over and done
Before we have even
        half begun
To do the things
        that we meant to do
But never have time
        to carry through—
And how nice it would be
        if we stopped to say
The things we feel
        in our hearts each day!

Every Day Is a Reason for Giving—and Giving Is the Key to Living!

So let us give "ourselves" away
Not just today but every day. . .
And remember a kind and thoughtful deed
Or a hand outstretched in time of need
Is the rarest of gifts, for it is a part
Not of the purse but a loving heart—
And he who gives of himself will find
True joy of heart and peace of mind.

Take Time to Be Kind

Kindness is a virtue
     given by THE LORD,
It pays dividends in happiness
     and joy is its reward. . .
For, if you practice kindness
     in all you say and do,
THE LORD will wrap HIS kindness
     around your heart and you. . .
And wrapped within HIS kindness
     you are sheltered and secure
And under HIS direction
     your way is safe and sure.

The Happiness
You Give Away Returns
to "Shine on You"

The MORE of everything you share,
The MORE you'll always have to spare. . .
For only what you GIVE AWAY
Enriches you from day to day!

The Language of the Heart

Just like a sunbeam brightens the sky,
A Smile on the face of a passerby
Can make a drab and crowded street
A pleasant place where Two Smiles meet.

In His Footsteps

WHEN SOMEONE DOES A KINDNESS
    IT ALWAYS SEEMS TO ME
THAT'S THE WAY GOD UP IN HEAVEN
    WOULD LIKE US ALL TO BE. . .
FOR WHEN WE BRING SOME PLEASURE
    TO ANOTHER HUMAN HEART,
WE HAVE FOLLOWED IN HIS FOOTSTEPS
    AND WE'VE HAD A LITTLE PART
IN SERVING HIM WHO LOVES US—
    FOR I AM VERY SURE IT'S TRUE
THAT IN SERVING THOSE AROUND US
    WE SERVE AND PLEASE HIM, TOO.

"Love One Another as I Have Loved You!"

"Love one another as I have loved you"
May seem impossible to do—
But if you will try to trust and believe
Great are the joys that you will receive . . .
For love makes us patient, understanding and kind,
And we judge with our hearts and not with our mind . . .
For as soon as love enters the heart's open door,
The faults we once saw are not there anymore,
And the things that seemed wrong begin to look right
When viewed in the softness of love's gentle light . . .
For love works in ways that are wondrous and strange,
And there is nothing in life that love cannot change,
And all that God promised will some day come true
When you love one another the way He loves You.

The Flower of Friendship

LIFE is like a GARDEN
And FRIENDSHIP like a FLOWER
That blooms and grows in beauty
With the sunshine and the shower. . .
And lovely are the blossoms
That are tended with great care
By those who work unselfishly
To make the place more fair. . .
And, like the GARDEN blossoms,
FRIENDSHIP'S FLOWER grows more sweet
When watched and tended carefully
By those we know and meet. . .
And, like sunshine adds new fragrance
And raindrops play their part,
Joy and sadness add new beauty
When there's FRIENDSHIP in the heart. . .
And, if the seed of FRIENDSHIP
Is planted deep and true
And watched with understanding,
FRIENDSHIP'S FLOWER WILL BLOOM FOR YOU.

A Prayer
for Those We Love

"OUR FATHER WHO ART IN HEAVEN,"
Hear this little prayer
And reach across the miles today
That stretch from HERE to THERE,
So I may feel much closer
To those I'm fondest of
And they may know I think of them
With thankfulness and love,
And help all people everywhere
Who must often dwell apart
To know that they're TOGETHER
In THE HAVEN of THE HEART!

What Is Love?

What is love?
No words can define it,
It's something so great
Only God could design it. . .
WONDER of WONDERS,
Beyond man's conception,
And only in God
Can love find true perfection,
For love is enduring
And patient and kind,
It judges all things
With the heart not the mind,

And love can transform
The most commonplace
Into beauty and splendor
And sweetness and grace. . .
For love is unselfish,
Giving more than it takes,
And no matter what happens
Love never forsakes,
It's faithful and trusting
And always believing,
Guileless and honest
And never deceiving. . .
Yes, love is beyond
What man can define,
For love is IMMORTAL
And God's Gift is DIVINE!

The Meaning
of True Love

It is sharing and caring,
Giving and forgiving,
Loving and being loved,
Walking hand in hand,
Talking heart to heart,
Seeing through each other's eyes,
Laughing together,
Weeping together,
Praying together,
And always trusting
And believing
And thanking GOD
For each other. . .
For love that is shared
       is a beautiful thing—
It enriches the soul
       and makes the heart sing!

The Gift of Lasting Love

Love is much more than a tender caress
    and more than bright hours of gay happiness,
For a lasting love is made up of sharing
    both hours that are "joyous" and also "despairing". . .
It's made up of patience and deep understanding
    and never of selfish and stubborn demanding,
It's made up of "CLIMBING THE STEEP HILLS TOGETHER"
    and facing with courage "LIFE'S STORMIEST WEATHER". . .
And nothing on earth or in heaven can part
    a love that has grown to be part of the heart,
And just like the sun and the stars and the sea,
    this love will go on through ETERNITY—
For "true love" lives on when earthly things die,
    for it's part of the SPIRIT that soars to the "SKY."

My Love for You

There are things we cannot measure,
Like the depths of waves and sea
And the heights of stars in heaven
And the joy YOU bring to me. . .
Like eternity's long endlessness
And the sunset's golden hue,
There is no way to measure
The love I have for YOU.

Each Day Brings
a Chance to Do Better

How often we wish for another chance
       to make a fresh beginning,
A chance to blot out our mistakes
       and change failure into winning—
And it does not take a special time
       to make a brand-new start,
It only takes the deep desire
       to try with all our heart
To live a little better
       and to always be forgiving
And to add a little "sunshine"
       to the world in which we're living—
So never give up in despair
       and think that you are through,
For there's always a tomorrow
       and a chance to start anew.

What Will You Do With This Day That's So New?

As we start a new day
    untouched and unmarred,
Unblemished and flawless,
    unscratched and unscarred,
May we try to do better
    and accomplish much more
And be kinder and wiser
    than in the day gone before—
Let us wipe our slates clean
    and start over again,
For GOD gives this privilege
    to all sincere men
Who will humbly admit
    they have failed many ways
But are willing to try
    and improve these "new days"
By asking GOD'S HELP
    in all that they do
And counting on HIM
    to refresh and renew
Their COURAGE and FAITH
    when things go wrong
And the way seems dark
    and the road rough and long—
WHAT WILL YOU DO
    WITH THIS DAY THAT'S SO NEW?
The choice is yours—
    GOD leaves that to YOU!

To Really Live
Is to Give and Forgive!

Since GOD forgives us,
       we, too, must forgive
And resolve to do better
       each day that we live
By constantly trying
       to be like HIM more nearly
And to trust in HIS wisdom
       and love HIM more dearly.

If You Haven't Succeeded, Maybe "New Management" Is Needed!

Nothing goes right,
>   everything's wrong,
You stumble and fall
>   as you trudge along,
The other guy wins,
>   but you always lose,
Whatever you hear
>   is always "bad news". . .
Well, here's some advice
>   that's worth a try,
Businessmen use it
>   when they want a "NEW HIGH"—
So "old management" goes
>   and the "new" comes in,
For this is the way
>   "BIG BUSINESS" CAN WIN. . .

So if you are trying
      to manage your life,
Yet all around
      is chaos and strife,
Make up your mind
      that you, too, need a change
And start making plans
      to somehow rearrange
The way that you think
      and the things that you do
And what are the things
      that are hindering you. . .
Then put yourself under
      GOD'S "MANAGEMENT" now,
And when HE takes over
      you'll find that somehow
Everything changes,
      "OLD THINGS PASS AWAY,"
And "the darkness of night"
      becomes "the brightness of day"—
For GOD can transform
      and change into "WINNERS"
The LOSERS, and SKEPTICS
      and even the SINNERS!

How to Find
Peace of Mind

We listen to the newscasts that come daily to our ears,
We read alarming headlines that intensify our fears,
We grow more and more dissatisfied and feel less and less secure
As our days become more anxious and the future more unsure—
For with violence and dissension and chaos all around
We no longer feel with certainty that we stand on solid ground—
But in place of reading headlines that disturb our peace of mind
We should once more read the BIBLE and on its pages we would find

That this age is no different from the millions gone before
And that in every hour of crisis God has opened up a door
To all who seek His guidance and trust His all-wise plan,
For God provides protection beyond that devised by man—
And while God's almighty power is not ours to understand,
We know Who Holds The Future and we know Who Holds Our Hand—
And to have the steadfast knowledge that we never walk alone
And to rest in the assurance that our every need is known
Will help dispel our worries and in trusting Him we'll find
Right in the midst of chaos God can give us Peace of Mind!

God of Creation
Save Our Nation

GREAT GOD THE FATHER OF ALL CREATION,
     LOOK DOWN UPON THIS STRIFE-TORN NATION,
REVIVE OUR SPIRITS LAIN DORMANT SO LONG,
     RENEW OUR FAITH AND KEEP IT STRONG,
FORGIVE OUR ARROGANCE AND GREED
     AND GUIDE US IN THIS HOUR OF NEED—
HAND OF GOD REACH OUT ONCE MORE
     AND WITH THE "BREATH OF LIFE" RESTORE
YOUR SPIRIT IN THE FLESH OF MEN
     SO WE MAY LIVE IN PEACE AGAIN—
FOR MANKIND'S FUTURE AND SURVIVAL
     DEPEND ALONE ON THE SPIRIT'S REVIVAL!

The Golden Years of Life

GOD in HIS LOVING
       AND ALL-WISE WAY
Makes the heart
       that once was young and gay
Serene and more gentle
       and less restless, too,
Content to remember
       the joys it once knew . . .
And all that we sought
       on "the pathway of pleasure"
Becomes but a memory
       to cherish and treasure—
The fast pace grows slower
       and the spirit serene,
And our souls can envision
       what our eyes have not seen. . .
And so while "LIFE'S SPRINGTIME"
       is sweet to recall,
The "AUTUMN OF LIFE"
       is THE BEST TIME of all,
For our wild, youthful yearnings
       all gradually cease
And GOD fills our days
       with BEAUTY and PEACE!

A Prayer of Thanks

Thank You, GOD, for everything
      I've experienced here on earth—
Thank You for protecting me
      from the moment of my birth—
And thank You for the beauty
      around me everywhere,
The gentle rain and glistening dew,
      the sunshine and the air,
The joyous gift of "feeling"
      the soul's soft, whispering voice
That speaks to me from deep within
      and makes my heart rejoice—
Oh, GOD, no words are great enough
      to thank You for just living,
And that is why every day
      is a day for real THANKSGIVING.

Show Me More Clearly the Way
To Serve and Love You
More Each Day

GOD, help me in my feeble way
To somehow do something each day
To show YOU that I love YOU best
And that my faith will stand each test
And let me serve YOU every day
And feel YOU near me when I pray. . .
Oh, hear my prayer, dear GOD above,
And MAKE ME WORTHY OF YOUR LOVE!

Inspiration!
Meditation!
Dedication!

Brighten your day
And lighten your way,
Lessen your cares
With DAILY PRAYERS,
Quiet your mind
And leave tension behind
And find inspiration
In "hushed meditation."

This Is All I Ask

LORD, show me the way
I can somehow repay
The blessings YOU'VE given to me. . .
LORD, teach me to do
What YOU most want me to
And to be what YOU want me to be . . .
I'm unworthy I know
But I do love YOU so—
I beg YOU to answer my plea. . .
I've not much to give
But as long as I live
May I give it completely to THEE!